Songbook of Absences

# SONGBOOK OF ABSENCES

## Selected Poems of MIGUEL HERNANDEZ

*Translations and Introduction by*
*Thomas C. Jones, Jr.*

Washington
The Charioteer Press
1980

THIS IS A *Charioteer Book.*

© 1972 *by Thomas C. Jones, Jr.*

*Library of Congress Catalog No. 72-91778*

*Published by The Charioteer Press.*

*Manufactured in the United States of America.*

SECOND PRINTING 1980.

These translations are for Caroline,
Elizabeth, and Tommy.

## ACKNOWLEDGMENTS

The publisher and the translator would like to thank Josefina Manresa, widow of Miguel Hernández and representative of his estate, for her cooperation.

The translator makes grateful acknowledgment to Jorge Ignacio Casteleiro and Keith Robert Krause for their many hours of invaluable assistance in preparing these translations. The translator would also like to thank Jorge Guitart and David Lagmanovich for their generous criticism of these translations in manuscript.

# CONTENTS

## INTRODUCTION

Miguel Hernández was thirty-one years old when he died in 1942. The work on which his reputation is based dates approximately from the outbreak of the Spanish Civil War in 1936. His poetry has influenced a generation of Hispanic poets, even though his mature creative life extended over a period of only six years, the last three in political prisons.* F. C. Sainz de Robles, one of Spain's leading critics, calls Hernández "the most extraordinary Spanish poet to emerge after 1934."

Miguel Hernández Gilabert was born October 30, 1910, in Orihuela in the province of Alicante. Almost entirely self-taught, he left school at the age of fifteen to help tend his father's small flock of goats and sheep. His first poem was published in a local weekly when he was twenty years old. Four years later, in 1934, he moved to Madrid, and by 1936 his work was appearing in Spain's leading literary magazines, drawing praise and encouragement from Juan Ramón Jiménez, García Lorca, Ortega y Gasset, Vicente Aleixandre, and Pablo Neruda, among others.

His early poems reflect the combined influences of Spanish classicism and modernism; his first masters included San Juan de la Cruz, Garcilaso, Rubén Darío, Quevedo, Bécquer, and, as with so many poets of his generation, Góngora. Of the prewar Spanish poets, he particularly admired Juan Ramón Jiménez, García Lorca, and Antonio Machado. But it was the poetry of Aleixandre and Neruda,

---

* As a result of his ardent support of the Loyalist struggle against Franco's forces, Hernández was imprisoned shortly after the end of the war in 1939. He originally received the death sentence, but this was commuted to thirty years' imprisonment.

his close friends and strong supporters,* that provided the bridge to his own unique voice. In Hernández's words:

> *With Vicente Aleixandre and Pablo Neruda*
> *I take my seat on the earth. . . .*

The central facts and events of his life—the death of his early mentor and closest friend, Ramón Sijé; his love for and marriage to Josefina Manresa; the birth, and death at age ten months, of his first son; the birth of a second son; his devotion to the Republic and the embittering experience of the war itself; and, finally, imprisonment under conditions that were to lead to his premature death from a pulmonary infection—these are the subjects of his poems. Hernández's interweaving of personal and social themes has influenced such poets as Blas de Otero, José Hierro, and José Angel Valente.

In his mature work Miguel Hernández confronts the themes of life and death and love, his chains of images giving breath to the most abstract ideas. When he cries

> *Aiii, life: what beautiful agony so near death!*

it is the cry of a man who confronted his tragic fate with dignity, passion, and courage.

THOMAS C. JONES, JR.

---

\* After Hernández's imprisonment, Neruda worked indefatigably from Paris to secure his friend's release. At least two of Hernández's biographers believe that the commutation of his death sentence was, in part at least, a result of Neruda's efforts.

Songbook of Absences

## XXIII

Como el toro he nacido para el luto
y el dolor, como el toro estoy marcado
por un hierro infernal en el costado
y por varón en la ingle con un fruto.

Como el toro lo encuentra diminuto
todo mi corazón desmesurado,
y del rostro del beso enamorado,
como el toro a tu amor se lo disputo.

Como el toro me crezco en el castigo,
la lengua en corazón tengo bañada
y llevo al cuello un vendaval sonoro.

Como el toro te sigo y te persigo,
y dejas mi deseo en una espada,
como el toro burlado, como el toro.

## SONNET XXIII

Like the bull I was born for mourning
and pain, like the bull I am marked
by an infernal brand on my side,
and, as a male, by a fruit in my groin.

Like the bull my deranged heart
finds everything too small,
and in love with a face and a kiss,
like the bull I must fight for your love.

Like the bull I thrive on punishment,
my tongue is bathed in my heart,
I wear a furious wind around my neck.

Like the bull I follow and chase you,
and you abandon my desire on a sword,
like the taunted bull, like the bull.

# ELEGIA

*(En Orihuela, su pueblo y el mío, se me ha muerto como del rayo Ramón Sijé, con quien tanto quería.)*

Yo quiero ser llorando el hortelano
de la tierra que ocupas y estercolas,
compañero del alma, tan temprano.

Alimentando lluvias, caracolas
y órganos mi dolor sin instrumento,
a las desalentadas amapolas

daré tu corazón por alimento.
Tanto dolor se agrupa en mi costado,
que por doler me duele hasta el aliento.

Un manotazo duro, un golpe helado,
un hachazo invisible y homicida,
un empujón brutal te ha derribado.

No hay extensión más grande que mi herida,
lloro mi desventura y sus conjuntos
y siento más tu muerte que mi vida.

Ando sobre rastrojos de difuntos,
y sin calor de nadie y sin consuelo
voy de mi corazón a mis asuntos.

Temprano levantó la muerte el vuelo,
temprano madrugó la madrugada,
temprano estás rodando por el suelo.

## ELEGY

*(In Orihuela, our hometown, Ramón Sijé, with whom I shared so much, was taken from me by death as if struck by lightning.)*

In mourning I want to be the keeper
of the earth you fill and enrich
so soon, companion of my soul.

Nourishing rains, seashells,
and organs with my impotent grief,
I shall feed your heart

to the dispirited poppies.
So much pain bunches up in my side
that it hurts even to breathe.

A hard fist, a frozen blow,
an invisible homicidal ax,
a brutal violent shove struck you down.

No space could be wider than my wound,
I mourn my misery and its allies,
I feel your death more than my life.

I walk over the stubble of the dead,
and, uncomforted, without warmth from anyone,
I go from my heart to my affairs.

How soon death raised its flight,
how early the dawn came,
how soon you are serving the earth.

No perdono a la muerte enamorada,
no perdono a la vida desatenta,
no perdono a la tierra ni a la nada.

En mis manos levanto una tormenta
de piedras, rayos y hachas estridentes
sedienta de catástrofes y hambrienta.

Quiero escarbar la tierra con los dientes,
quiero apartar la tierra parte a parte
a dentelladas secas y calientes.

Quiero minar la tierra hasta encontrarte
y besarte la noble calavera
y desmordazarte y regresarte.

Volverás a mi huerto y a mi higuera:
por los altos andamios de las flores
pajareará tu alma colmenera

de angelicales ceras y labores.
Volverás al arrullo de las rejas
de los enamorados labradores.

Alegrarás la sombra de mis cejas,
y tu sangre se irá a cada lado
disputando tu novia y las abejas.

Tu corazón, ya terciopelo ajado,
llama a un campo de almendras espumosas
mi avariciosa voz de enamorado.

A las aladas almas de las rosas
del almendro de nata te requiero,
que tenemos que hablar de muchas cosas,
compañero del alma, compañero.

*(10 de enero de 1936)*

6

I do not pardon death its love,
I do not pardon life its carelessness,
I pardon neither the earth nor nothingness itself.

In my hands I raise a storm
of stones, lightning, and strident axes,
thirsting after catastrophes, hungering.

I want to dig into the earth with my teeth,
I want to break up the earth bit by bit
with hot, dry bites.

I want to burrow in the earth until I find you
and kiss your noble skull
and unchoke you and bring you back.

You will return to my orchard, my fig tree:
in the high scaffolds of the flowers
your soul will wander, gathering

angelic wax and honey from its hives.
You will return to the lullaby of the plows
of fieldhands in love.

You will gladden the shadow over my eyes,
and your blood will flow, reaching out
both to the bees and to the woman you love.

My voice, greedy with love, is calling
your heart, already faded velvet,
to a field of almond blossoms.

I summon you to the frosted almond tree
to the winged souls of the roses:
we have so many things we have to talk about,
you, my companion, companion of my soul.

(*January 10, 1936*)

7

## EL SUDOR

En el mar halla el agua su paraíso ansiado
y el sudor su horizonte, su fragor, su plumaje.
El sudor es un árbol desbordante y salado,
un voraz oleaje.

Llega desde la edad del mundo más remota
a ofrecer a la tierra su copa sacudida,
a sustentar la sed y la sal gota a gota,
a iluminar la vida.

Hijo del movimiento, primo del sol, hermano
de la lágrima, deja rodando por las eras,
del abril al octubre, del invierno al verano,
áureas enredaderas.

Cuando los campesinos van por la madrugada
a favor de la esteva removiendo el reposo,
se visten una blusa silenciosa y dorada
de sudor silencioso.

Vestidura de oro de los trabajadores,
adorno de las manos como de las pupilas.
Por la atmósfera esparce sus fecundos olores
una lluvia de axilas.

El sabor de la tierra se enriquece y madura:
caen los copos del llanto laborioso y oliente,
maná de los varones y de la agricultura,
bebida de mi frente.

## *SWEAT*

In the sea, water finds the paradise it longs for,
and sweat, its horizon, its tumult, its plumage.
Sweat is a tree, overflowing and salty,
a voracious succession of waves.

It arrives from the world's most remote age
to offer the earth its trembling glass,
to nourish thirst and salt drop by drop,
to illuminate life.

Child of movement, cousin of the sun, brother
of the tear, it goes rolling through the fields
from April to October, from winter to summer
—streams of golden vines.

When farmers move through the dawn
trailing the plow that robs them of sleep,
they wear a silent, golden blouse
of hushed sweat.

Golden dress of the workers,
jewel of the hands and the eyes:
it spreads fertile odors through thin air,
a rain from armpits.

The flavor of the earth grows rich and matures:
snowflakes fall from the odorous, toilsome weeping,
manna from males and agriculture,
drink of my forehead.

Los que no habéis sudado jamás, los que andáis yertos
en el ocio sin brazos, sin música, sin poros,
no usaréis la corona de los poros abiertos
ni el poder de los toros.

Viviréis maloliendo, moriréis apagados:
la encendida hermosura reside en los talones
de los cuerpos que mueven sus miembros trabajados
como constelaciones.

Entregad al trabajo, compañeros, las frentes:
que el sudor, con su espada de sabrosos cristales,
con sus lentos diluvios, os hará transparentes,
venturosos, iguales.

You who have never sweated, you who walk stiffly
in a leisure without arms, without music, without pores,
never will you wear the crown of open pores,
nor the power of the bulls.

You will live stinking, you will die extinguished:
inflamed beauty resides in the heels
of those who must move their limbs,
their bodies wrought like constellations.

My brothers, surrender your foreheads to work:
for your sweat, with its sword of salty crystals,
with its gentle floods, will make you transparent,
joyous, equal.

## CANCION PRIMERA

Se ha retirado el campo
al ver abalanzarse
crispadamente al hombre.

¡Qué abismo entre el olivo
y el hombre se descubre!

El animal que canta:
el animal que puede
llorar y echar raíces,
rememoró sus garras.

Garras que revestía
de suavidad y flores,
pero que, al fin, desnuda
en toda su crueldad.

Crepitan en mis manos.
Aparta de ellas, hijo.
Estoy dispuesto a hundirlas,
dispuesto a proyectarlas
sobre tu carne leve.

He regresado al tigre.
Aparta o te destrozo.

Hoy el amor es muerte,
y el hombre acecha al hombre.

## FIRST SONG

Seeing the man's
convulsive charge,
the countryside retreated.

What an abyss laid open
between olive tree and man!

The animal that sings:
the animal that can
weep and take root
remembered his claws.

Claws that he dressed
in softness and flowers,
but which, in the end, he bares
in all of his cruelty.

They crackle in my hands.
Keep back from them, child.
I am ready to sink them,
ready to hurl them
toward your light flesh.

I have regressed to the tiger.
Keep back or I'll tear you apart.

Today love is death,
and man lies in ambush for man.

## CANCION ULTIMA

Pintada, no vacía:
pintada está mi casa
del color de las grandes
pasiones y desgracias.

Regresará del llanto
adonde fue llevada
con su desierta mesa,
con su ruinosa cama.

Florecerán los besos
sobre las almohadas.
Y en torno de los cuerpos
elevará la sábana
su intensa enredadera
nocturna, perfumada.

El odio se amortigua
detrás de la ventana.

Será la garra suave.

Dejadme la esperanza.

## LAST SONG

Painted, but not empty:
my house is painted
with the color of the great
passions and tragedies.

It will come back from the weeping
where it was carried
with its deserted table,
with its ruinous bed.

Kisses will bloom
on the pillows.
And wrapped around the bodies
the sheet will raise
it's immense perfumed
nocturnal vine.

Hatred subsides
on the other side of the window.

The claw will be smooth.

Allow me this hope.

15

Ausencia en todo veo:
tus ojos la reflejan.

Ausencia en todo escucho:
tu voz a tiempo suena.

Ausencia en todo aspiro:
tu aliento huele a hierba.

Ausencia en todo toco:
tu cuerpo se despuebla.

Ausencia en todo siento.
Ausencia. Ausencia. Ausencia.

## *ABSENCE*

Absence in all I see:
your eyes reflect it.

Absence in all I hear:
your voice strikes on time.

Absence in all I breathe:
your breath smells of grass.

Absence in all I touch:
your body devastates itself.

Absence in all I feel.
Absence. Absence. Absence.

Una fotografía.

Un cartón expresivo,
envuelto por los meses
en los rincones íntimos.

Un agua de distancia
quiero beber: gozar
un fondo de fantasma.

Un cartón me conmueve.

Un cartón me acompaña.

## PHOTOGRAPH

A photograph.

Expressive cardboard,
wrapped by the months
in the innermost corners.

A water of distance
I want to drink—to savor
an apparition's depth.

Cardboard touches me.

Cardboard goes with me.

19

Rumorosas pestañas
de los cañaverales.
Cayendo sobre el sueño
del hombre hasta dejarle
el pecho apaciguado
y la cabeza suave.

Ahogad la voz del arma,
que no despierte y salte
con el cuchillo de odio
que entre sus dientes late.

Así, dormido, el hombre
toda la tierra vale.

## MURMURING EYELASHES

Murmuring eyelashes
of the canefields.
Settling over sleep
leaving a man with
his breast calmed
his mind at rest.

Smother the weapon's voice
don't let him waken and leap
with the knife of hatred
throbbing between his teeth.

Lying there, asleep, a man is worth
the entire earth.

El mundo es como aparece
ante mis cinco sentidos,
y ante los tuyos que son
las orillas de los míos.
El mundo de los demás
no es el nuestro: no es el mismo.
Lecho del agua que soy,
tú, los dos, somos el río
donde cuando más profundo
se ve más despacio y límpido.
Imágenes de la vida:
a la vez que recibimos,
nos reciben entregadas
más unidamente a un ritmo.
Pero las cosas se forman
con nuestros propios delirios.
El aire tiene el tamaño
del corazón que respiro
y el sol es como la luz
con que yo le desafío.
Ciego para los demás,
oscuros, siempre remisos,
miramos siempre hacia adentro,
vemos desde lo más íntimo.
Trabajo y amor me cuesta
conmigo así, ver contigo;
aparecer, como el agua
con la arena, siempre unidos.
Nadie me verá del todo
ni es nadie como lo miro.
Somos algo más que vemos,
algo menos que inquirimos.

## THE WORLD IS THE WAY
## IT APPEARS

The world is the way it appears
before my five senses,
and before yours, which are
the shores of mine.
The world of others
is not ours: it is not the same.
You are the bed of the stream that I am,
and together we are the river
that is seen clearer and slower
as it deepens.
Images of life:
they receive us
as we receive them
merged into rhythm.
But things take their form
from our own delirium.
Air has the dimensions
of the heart I breathe
and the sun is like the light
with which I challenge it.
Blind toward others,
obscure and always remiss,
we always look inward,
we see from the most intimate.
It cost me labor and love
to see what you see;
to appear, like water
with sand, always united.
No one will see all of me
nor is anyone as I view him.
We are something more than we see,
something less than we search for.

Algún suceso de todos
pasa desapercibido.
Nadie nos ha visto. A nadie
ciegos de ver, hemos visto.

Certain events of the whole
pass unguarded.
No one has seen us. We have seen
no one, blind as we are, from seeing.

El cementerio está cerca
de donde tú y yo dormimos,
entre nopales azules,
pitas azules y niños
que gritan vívidamente
si un muerto nubla el camino.

De aquí al cementerio, todo
es azul, dorado, límpido.
Cuatro pasos y los muertos.
Cuatro pasos y los vivos.

Límpido, azul y dorado,
se hace allí remoto el hijo.

## THE CEMETERY

The cemetery is near
the place where we sleep,
between blue nopals,
blue pitas and children
that cry vividly
if a corpse clouds the path.

From here to the cemetery, all
is blue, golden, limpid.
Four steps and the dead.
Four steps and the living.

Limpid, blue and golden,
my son becomes remote there.

# EL ULTIMO RINCON

El último y el primero:
rincón para el sol más grande,
sepultura de esta vida
donde tus ojos no caben.
Allí quisiera tenderme
para desenamorarme.
Por el olivo lo quiero,
lo percibo por la calle,
se sume por los rincones
donde su sumen los árboles.
Se ahonda y hace más honda
la intensidad de mi sangre.
Carne de mi movimiento,
huesos de ritmos mortales,
me muero por respirar
sobre vuestros ademanes.
Corazón que entre dos piedras
ansiosas de machacarle,
de tanto querer te ahogas
como un mar entre dos mares.
De tanto querer me ahogo,
y no es posible ahogarme.
¿Qué hice para que pusieran
a mi vida tanta cárcel?
Tu pelo donde lo negro
ha sufrido las edades
de la negrura más firme,
y la más emocionante:

## THE LAST CORNER

The last and the first:
corner for the largest sun,
tomb of this life
where your eyes do not fit.
There I would like to lie down
to fall out of love.
I want it near the olive tree,
I sense it in the street,
it sinks in the corners
where the trees are sinking.
It penetrates and deepens
the intensity of my blood.
Flesh of my movement,
bones of mortal rhythms,
I die so as to breathe
over your gestures.
Heart between two stones
anxious to crush it,
you drown from so much longing
like a sea between two seas.
I drown from so much longing,
it is impossible to drown.
What have I done that they covered
my life with so much prison?
Your hair where black
has suffered the ages
of the most unchanging
the most arousing blackness:

tu secular pelo negro
recorro hasta remontarme
a la negrura primera
de tus ojos y tus padres;
al rincón del pelo denso
donde relampagueaste.
Ay, el rincón de tu vientre;
el callejón de tu carne:
el callejón sin salida
donde agonicé una tarde.
La pólvora y el amor
marchan sobre las ciudades
deslumbrando, removiendo
la población de la sangre.
El naranjo sabe a vida
y el olivo a tiempo sabe
y entre el clamor de los dos
mi corazón se debate.
El último y el primero:
náufrago rincón, estanque
de saliva detenida
sobre su amoroso cauce.
Siesta que ha entenebrecido
el sol de las humedades.
Allí quisiera tenderme
para desenamorarme.
Después del amor, la tierra.
Después de la tierra, nadie.

I go over and over your ageless
black hair until I reach
the first blackness
of your eyes and your ancestors,
to the corner of dense hair
where you flashed like lightning.
Aiii, the corner of your womb;
the passage of your flesh:
the dead end
where I agonized one afternoon.
Dust and love
march across the cities
dazzling and stirring
the population of the blood.
The orange tree tastes of life,
the olive tree tastes of time,
and my heart debates
between their outcries.
The last and the first:
shipwrecked corner, pool
of spit imprisoned
over its loving riverbed.
Siesta darkened by
the sun of dampnesses.
There I would like to lie down
to fall out of love.
After love, the earth.
After the earth, no one.

# HIJO DE LA LUZ Y DE LA SOMBRA

## I

(HIJO DE LA SOMBRA)

Eres la noche, esposa: la noche en el instante
mayor de su potencia lunar y femenina.
Eres la medianoche: la sombra culminante
donde culmina el sueño, donde el amor culmina.

Forjado por el día, mi corazón que quema
lleva su gran pisada de sol adonde quieres,
con un sólido impulso, con una luz suprema,
cumbre de las mañanas y los atardeceres.

Daré sobre tu cuerpo cuando la noche arroje
su avaricioso anhelo de imán y poderío.
Un astral sentimiento febril me sobrecoge,
incendia mi osamenta con un escalofrío.

El aire de la noche desordena tus pechos,
y desordena y vuelca los cuerpos con su choque.
Como una tempested de enloquecidos lechos,
eclipsa las parejas, las hace un solo bloque.

La noche se ha encendido como una sorda hoguera
de llamas minerales y oscuras embestidas.
Y alrededor la sombra late como si fuera
las almas de los pozos y el vino difundidas.

Ya la sombra es el nido cerrado, incandescente,
la visible ceguera puesta sobre quien ama;
ya provoca el abrazo cerrado, ciegamente,
ya recoge en sus cuevas cuanto la luz derrama.

# CHILD OF THE LIGHT AND THE SHADOW

## I

### (CHILD OF THE SHADOW)

My love, you are night: night at the peak
of its lunar, feminine force.
You are midnight: the culminating spirit
where dream, and love, culminate.

Forged by sunlight, my fiery heart
bears the sun's huge imprint wherever you wish,
with an urgent thrust, a supreme blaze,
summit of mornings and evenings.

When the night projects its greedy desire,
its magnetic pulse, I will invade your body.
A feverish astral sadness chills me,
inflaming my bones with shivering.

The night air disturbs your breasts,
with its shock it disturbs and capsizes bodies.
Like a tempest of maddened beds,
it eclipses lovers, turning them into a block of stone.

The night has ignited like a deaf bonfire
of mineral flames and dark assaults.
All around the shadow throbs, as if it were
the diffused souls of wells and wine.

Now the shadow is the closed nest, incandescent,
visible blindness lowered over whoever loves;
now it provokes the closed embrace, blindly,
now it gathers in its caves all that the light pours out.

La sombra pide, exige seres que se entrelacen,
besos que la constelen de relámpagos largos,
bocas embravecidas, batidas, que atenacen,
arrullos que hagan música de sus mudos letargos.

Pide que nos echemos tú y yo sobre la manta,
tú y yo sobre la luna, tú y yo sobre la vida.
Pide que tú y yo ardamos fundiendo en la garganta,
con todo el firmamento, la tierra estremecida.

El hijo está en la sombra que acumula luceros,
amor, tuétano, luna, claras oscuridades.
Brota de sus perezas y de sus agujeros,
y de sus solitarias y apagadas ciudades.

El hijo está en la sombra: de la sombra ha surtido,
y a su origen infunden los astros una siembra,
un zumo lácteo, un flujo de cálido latido,
que ha de obligar sus huesos al sueño y a la hembra.

Moviendo está la sombra sus fuerzas siderales,
tendiendo está la sombra su constelada umbría,
volcando las parejas y haciéndolas nupciales.
Tú eres la noche, esposa. Yo soy el mediodía.


## II

(HIJO DE LA LUZ)

Tú eres el alba, esposa: la principal penumbra,
recibes entornadas las horas de tu frente.
Decidido al fulgor, pero entornado, alumbra
tu cuerpo. Tus entrañas forjan el sol naciente.

The shadow begs, and needs, beings that interlace,
kisses that form constellations of prolonged lightning,
enraged mouths, beaten, that tear at the flesh,
lullabies that turn its mute lethargy into music.

It begs that we throw ourselves, you and I, toward the
  blanket,
toward the moon, toward life.
It begs that we burn, melting in our throats
the trembling earth with all the firmament.

The child is in the shadow that gathers morning stars,
love, marrow, moonlight, clear darknesses.
He surges from their sloth and their holes,
from their lonely, extinguished cities.

The child is in the shadow: he spurts from the shadow,
and stars infuse a sowing at his source,
a milky sap, a flow of warm throbbing
that binds his bones to the dream and to the female.

The shadow is moving its sidereal forces,
forming its dark constellations,
capsizing lovers and joining them.
You are night, my love. I am midday.

## II

### (CHILD OF THE LIGHT)

You are dawn, my love: the first twilight,
your face is lighted by the half-closed hours.
Committed to brilliance, but half-closed, your body
gives light. Your womb forges the rising sun.

35

Centro de claridades, la gran hora te espera
en el umbral de un fuego que al fuego mismo abrasa:
te espero yo, inclinado como el trigo a la era,
colocando en el centro de la luz nuestra casa.

La noche desprendida de los pozos oscuros,
se sumerge en los pozos donde ha echado raíces.
Y tú te abres al parto luminoso, entre muros
que se rasgan contigo como pétreas matrices.

La gran hora del parto, la más rotunda hora:
estallan los relojes sintiendo tu alarido,
se abren todas las puertas del mundo, de la aurora,
y el sol nace en tu vientre donde encontró su nido.

El hijo fue primero sombra y ropa cosida
por tu corazón hondo desde tus hondas manos.
Con sombras y con ropas anticipó su vida,
con sombras y con ropas de gérmenes humanos.

Las sombras y las ropas sin población, desiertas,
se han poblado de un niño sonoro, un movimiento,
que en nuestra casa pone de par en par las puertas,
y ocupa en ella a gritos el luminoso asiento.

¡Ay, la vida: qué hermoso penar tan moribundo!
Sombras y ropas trajo la del hijo que nombras.
Sombras y ropas llevan los hombres por el mundo.
Y todos dejan siempre sombras: ropas y sombras.

Hijo del alba eres, hijo del mediodía.
Y ha de quedar de tí luces en todo impuestas,
mientras tu madre y yo vamos a la agonía,
dormidos y despiertos con el amor a cuestas.

Center of brightness, the great hour awaits you
on the threshold of a fire that burns the fire itself:
bent like the wheat to the threshing floor, I wait for you,
arranging our house in the center of the light.

The generous night of the dark wells
sinks in the wells where it has taken root.
And you open yourself to luminous childbirth,
between walls, stone matrices, torn as you are torn.

The great hour of childbirth, the most spherical hour:
hearing your scream, the clocks explode,
all the doors of the world, of daybreak, fly open,
and the sun is born in your womb, where it found its nest.

At first the child was shadow and cloth,
sewn in the depths of your heart, of your hands.
With shadows and cloth he anticipated his life,
with shadows and cloth of human seeds.

Empty, deserted shadows and cloth
have been filled with a sonorous boy, a movement,
that throws wide open the doors of our house,
while a luminous order fills it with cries.

Aiii, life: what beautiful agony so near death!
Shadows and cloth bore the life of the child you name.
Men wear shadows and cloth through the world.
And everyone always leaves shadows: cloth and shadows.

You are child of the dawn, child of midday.
And you will leave light imposed on everything,
while your mother and I are moving toward agony,
asleep and awake with love in our care.

Hablo, y el corazón me sale en el aliento.
Si no hablara lo mucho que quiero me ahogaría.
Como espliego y resinas perfumo tu aposento.
Tú eres el alba, esposa. Yo soy el mediodía.


## III

(HIJO DE LA LUZ Y DE LA SOMBRA)

Tejidos en el alba, grabados, dos panales
no pueden detener la miel en los pezones.
Tus pechos en el alba: maternos manantiales,
luchan y se atropellan con blancas efusiones.

Se han desbordado, esposa, lunarmente tus venas,
hasta inundar la casa que tu sabor rezuma.
Y es como si brotaras de un pueblo de colmenas,
tú toda una colmena de leche con espuma.

Es como si tu sangre fuera dulzura toda,
laboriosas abejas filtradas por tus poros.
Oigo un clamor de leche, de inundación, de boda
junto a tí, recorrida por caudales sonoros.

Caudalosa mujer: en tu vientre me entierro.
Tu caudaloso vientre será mi sepultura.
Si quemaran mis huesos con la llama del hierro,
verían qué grabada llevo allí tu figura.

Para siempre fundidos en el hijo quedamos:
fundidos como anhelan nuestras ansias voraces:
en un ramo de tiempo, de sangre, los dos ramos,
en un haz de caricias, de pelo, los dos haces.

I speak, and my heart goes out in my breath.
If I could not say how much I love, I would drown.
I perfume your room with lavender and resins.
You are dawn, my love. I am midday.

## III

(CHILD OF THE LIGHT AND THE SHADOW)

Carved, woven in the dawn, two honeycombs
cannot hold back the honey in their nipples.
Your breasts in the dawn: maternal springs
struggle and rush with white effusions.

Your veins have overflowed, my love, like the moon,
inundating the house your fragrance fills,
as if you surged from a village of beehives,
you a whole beehive of milk with foam.

As if your blood were all sweetness,
laborious bees filtered through your pores.
I hear a clamor of milk, of inundation, of the wedding
beside you, covered with abundant sounds.

Abundant woman: I bury myself in your womb.
Your abundant womb will be my grave.
If my bones burned with the flame of iron,
they would see that I wear your form etched there.

We remain forever melted together in our child:
a fusion our longing voraciously desires:
our two bouquets in one bouquet of time, of blood,
our two clusters in one cluster of caresses, of hair.

Los muertos, con un fuego congelado que abrasa,
laten junto a los vivos de una manera terca.
Viene a ocupar el hijo los campos y la casa
que tú y yo abandonamos quedándonos muy cerca.

Haremos de este hijo generador sustento,
y hará de nuestra carne materia decisiva:
donde sientan su alma las manos y el aliento
las hélices circulen, la agricultura viva.

El hará que esta vida no caiga derribada,
pedazo desprendido de nuestros dos pedazos,
que de nuestras dos bocas hará una sola espada
y dos brazos eternos de nuestros cuatro brazos.

No te quiero a tí sola: te quiero en tu ascendencia
y en cuanto de tu vientre descenderá mañana.
Porque la especie humana me han dado por herencia,
la familia del hijo será la especie humana.

Con el amor a cuestas, dormidos y despiertos,
seguiremos besándonos en el hijo profundo.
Besándonos tú y yo se besan nuestros muertos,
se besan los primeros pobladores del mundo.

(*1938*)

The dead, with a frozen fire that burns,
throb stubbornly next to the living:
the child is coming to occupy the fields and the house
that you and I are leaving, though we stay close by.

We will make this child a generative force,
and he will make final matter of our flesh:
where his hands and his heart set down his soul,
propellers will whirl, crops will thrive.

Fragment torn loose from our two fragments,
he will assure that this life is not wasted,
of our two mouths he will make one sword,
and of our four arms, two eternal arms.

I do not love you alone: I love you in your forefathers,
and in all that will descend from your womb tomorrow.
Because they have given me mankind as a heritage,
the family of the child will be mankind.

With love in our care, asleep and awake,
we will continue to kiss in the deep child.
As we kiss each other, our dead are kissing,
the first populators of the world are kissing.

*(1938)*

41

## SEPULTURA DE LA IMAGINACION

Un albañil quería . . . No le faltaba aliento.
Un albañil quería, piedra tras piedra, muro
tras muro, levantar una imagen al viento
desencadenador en el futuro.

Quería un edificio capaz de lo más leve.
No le faltaba aliento. ¡Cuánto aquel ser quería!
Piedras de plumas, muros de pájaros los mueve
una imaginación al mediodía.

Reía. Trabajaba. Cantaba. De sus brazos,
con un poder más alto que el ala de los truenos,
iban brotando muros lo mismo que aletazos.
Pero los aletazos duran menos.

Al fin, era la piedra su agente. Y la montaña
tiene valor de vuelo si es totalmente activa.
Piedra por piedra es peso y hunde cuanto acompaña
aunque esto sea un mundo de ansia viva.

Un albañil quería . . . Pero la piedra cobra
su torva densidad brutal en un momento.
Aquel hombre labraba su cárcel. Y en su obra
fueron precipitados él y el viento.

## TOMB OF THE IMAGINATION

A stonemason wanted . . . he dared to want. . . .
A stonemason wanted, stone upon stone,
wall after wall, to raise an image to the wind,
to the unchaining wind of the future.

He wanted a structure capable of the ethereal.
He dared to want. How deeply he wanted!
An imagination lifted stones made of feathers,
walls made of birds, toward the south wind.

He laughed. He worked. He sang. Walls
like wingbeats flew from his arms
with a force greater than the wing of thunder.
But wingbeats don't last so long.

Finally, stone was his agent. And a mountain
that never rests has the power to fly.
Stone by stone it weighs down and crushes
all it encloses, even a world of living desire.

A stonemason wanted. . . . But stone recovers
its grim brutal density in an instant.
That man worked on his own prison. And in his work
he and the wind were driven headlong.

## ASCENCION DE LA ESCOBA

Coronada la escoba de laurel, mirto, rosa,
es el héroe entre aquellos que afrontan la basura.
Para librar del polvo sin vuelo cada cosa
bajó, porque era palma y azul, desde la altura.

Su ardor de espada joven y alegre no reposa.
Delgada de ansiedad, pureza, sol, bravura,
azucena que barre sobre la misma fosa,
es cada vez más alta, más cálida, más pura.

¡Nunca! La escoba nunca será crucificada,
porque la juventud propaga su esqueleto
que es una sola flauta, muda, pero sonora.

Es una sola lengua sublime y acordada.
Y ante su aliento raudo se ausenta el polvo quieto,
y asciende una palmera, columna hacia la aurora.

*(Cárcel de Torrijos. Septiembre de 1939)*

## ASCENSION OF THE BROOM*

Crowned with laurel, myrtle, rose, the broom
is hero to those who confront the refuse.
It descended from the summit—because it was a palm leaf,
and blue—to free each thing from flightless dust.

Its passion of a young and happy sword never rests.
Lean with anxiety, purity, sun, courage,
white lily that sweeps the grave itself,
it grows taller, warmer, purer.

Never! The broom will never be crucified,
because youth propagates its frame,
which is a lone flute, mute but sonorous.

It is a lone flute sublimely tuned.
And before its rapid breath the quiet dust disappears
and ascends a palm tree, column toward dawn.

(*Torrijos Prison. September 1939*)

---

* Hernández had been forced to sweep the prison as a punishment.

# NANAS DE LA CEBOLLA

*(Dedicadas a su hijo, a raíz de recibir una carta de su mujer, en la que le decía que no comía más que pan y cebolla.)*

La cebolla es escarcha
cerrada y pobre.
Escarcha de tus días
y de mis noches.
Hambre y cebolla,
hielo negro y escarcha
grande y redonda.

En la cuna del hambre
mi niño estaba.
Con sangre de cebolla
se amamantaba.
Pero tu sangre,
escarchada de azúcar,
cebolla y hambre.

Una mujer morena
resuelta en luna
se derrama hilo a hilo
sobre la cuna.
Ríete, niño,
que te tragas la luna
cuando es preciso.

## LULLABY OF THE ONION

*(Dedicated to his son after receiving a
letter from his wife saying that she had
only bread and onion to eat.)*

The onion is frost,
cloudy and poor.
Frost of your days
and my nights.
Hunger and onion,
black ice and frost,
huge and round.

My child was lying
in the cradle of hunger.
He nursed
on the blood of the onion.
But your blood,
frosted with sugar,
onion and hunger.

Dissolve in moonlight
a brown-haired woman
overflows, drop by drop,
over the cradle.
Laugh, little boy,
drink of the moon
whenever you must.

47

Alondra de mi casa,
ríete mucho.
Es tu risa en tus ojos
la luz del mundo.
Ríete tanto
que mi alma al oírte
bata el espacio.

Tu risa me hace libre,
me pone alas.
Soledades me quita,
cárcel me arranca.
Boca que vuela,
corazón que en tus labios
relampaguea.

Es tu risa la espada
más victoriosa,
vencedor de las flores
y las alondras.
Rival del sol.
Porvenir de mis huesos
y de mi amor.

La carne aleteante,
súbito el párpado,
el vivir como nunca
coloreado.
¡Cuánto jilguero
se remonta, aletea,
desde tu cuerpo!

Lark of my house,
laugh often.
The laughter in your eyes
is the light of the world.
Laugh so much
that my soul, hearing you,
annihilates distance.

You laughter frees me,
giving me wings.
It lifts away my loneliness,
demolishes my prison.
Mouth that flies,
heart that touches your lips
with lightning.

Your laughter frees me,
victorious sword,
conqueror of flowers
and larks.
Rival of the sun.
Future of my bones,
of my love.

The quivering flesh,
the sudden eyelid,
life more flushed
than ever before.
How many linnets
soar, flutter
from your body!

Desperté de ser niño:
nunca despiertes.
Triste llevo la boca:
ríete siempre.
Siempre en la cuna,
defendiendo la risa
pluma por pluma.

Ser de vuelo tan alto,
tan extendido,
que tu carne es el cielo
recién nacido.
¡Si yo pudiera
remontarme al origen
de tu carrera!

Al octavo mes ríes
con cinco azahares.
Con cinco diminutas
ferocidades.
Con cinco dientes
como cinco jazmines
adolescentes.

Frontera de los besos
serán mañana,
cuando en la dentadura
sientas un arma.
Sientas un fuego
correr dientes abajo
buscando el centro.

I awoke from being a child:
never awaken.
I have a sad mouth:
laugh always.
Always in the cradle
defending laughter
feather by feather.

Fly so high,
so far,
that your flesh is the sky
newborn.
If only I could soar
back to the beginning
of your flight.

In the eighth month you laugh
with five orange blossoms.
With five small
furies.
With five teeth
like five adolescent
jasmins.

Tomorrow they will be the frontier
of kisses,
when you feel your teeth
as a weapon,
when you feel a fire
flowing down through your teeth
searching for the center.

Vuela niño en la doble
luna del pecho:
él, triste de cebolla,
tú, satisfecho.
No te derrumbes.
No sepas lo que pasa
ni lo que ocurre.

Fly, little boy, on the double
moon of the breast:
it, sad with onion;
you, satisfied, content.
Hold back.
Ignore what happens
and what goes on.

*This book was composed on the Linotype
in No. 7 and printed by
Theo. Gaus, Ltd., Brooklyn, N.Y. 11201.*